EXPLORING HISTORY

The Thirties

Books are to be returned on or before
the last date below.

LIBREX —

Oliver & Boyd
Robert Stevenson House
1–3 Baxter's Place
Leith Walk
Edinburgh EHI 3BB
A division of Longman Group Ltd.

First published 1984

ISBN 0 05 003673 4

Set in 12/14pt Times Roman and
Gill Sans

Printed in Hong Kong by
Commonwealth Printing Press Ltd.

Horse-drawn and motor traffic
crowded the streets in the 1930s.
Look for a clue in the picture
which tells you which city this is.

Acknowledgments

The author and publishers would like to thank the following for
permission to reprint copyright material:
Extracts
Allison & Busby: *Jarrow March* by T. Pickard; BBC Publications:
Chelsea Child by Rose Gamble; The Literary Executors of Vera
Brittain: *Testament of Experience* by Vera Brittain; Cambridge
University Press: *Men Without Work* (Pilgrim Trust); Aidan
Crawley: *Looking for Trouble* by Virginia Cowles; David & Charles
Ltd: *Later Than We Thought* by Rene Cutforth; Victor Gollancz
Ltd: *Hungry England* by Fenner Brockway; A M Heath & Co.
Ltd. on behalf of the estate of the late Sonia Orwell: *The Road
to Wigan Pier* by George Orwell (Published by Martin Secker &
Warburg Ltd.); William Heinemann Ltd: *English Journey* by J.B.
Priestley (first published by William Heinemann Ltd, 1934); David
Higham Associates Ltd: *I Am My Brother* by John Lehmann
(published by Longman), and *You May Well Ask* by Naomi
Mitchison; Hutchinson Publishing Group Ltd: *The Billy Butlin Story*
by Billy Butlin (published by Jorrolds), and *Best Foot Forward* by
Molly Weir; Macmillan Publishing Co. Inc. *My Life in Service* by
Rosina Harrison (published by Cassell); Martin Secker & Warburg
Ltd: *Speak for England* by Melvin Bragg.
Illustrations (on the pages indicated)
BBC Hulton Picture Library 5, 9, 11, 13, 14, 15, 17 (bottom),
20, 28 (left and right), 30 (top and bottom), 35, 36 (top and
bottom), 39; Greater London Council 25; *Illustrated London
News* Picture Library 10, 22 (left); Keystone Press Agency Ltd
12, 19, 22 (right), 26, 34 (top), 38; Kodak Museum 31; London
Transport Executive, *cover*; Marks & Spencer plc 18; Popperfoto
37; Science Museum (Crown Copyright) 33; Topham 2, 3, 4, 7,
16, 17 (top), 23, 24, 27, 34 (bottom).
While every effort has been made to trace copyright owners,
apologies are made for any omissions in the above list.

Contents

Introduction

1. Look at the pictures below and opposite. Write out as many clues as possible that tell you that neither of them is a modern scene.

These pictures give glimpses of life in Britain in the Thirties. In the following pages you will be able to find out more about how people lived then. Some clues can be found in the pictures that were taken then and some in what was written at that time. Other clues lie in people's memories, when they look back on their earlier lives.

Life in Britain then was very different from life today. Yet the 1930s are not in the distant past; many people alive today can remember them. Try and find out more by exploring the area where you live.

Interview people who can remember the 1930s. Your relatives and neighbours may be able to provide you with a great deal of information. Work out the questions that you want to ask before you go. Record the interview if possible. It is probably best to begin by finding out about ordinary everyday life. Plan questions about schooldays, meals, clothes, travel, entertainments, holidays and work. Later questions may be about important events, and especially about the coming of war.

Some people may have kept photographs that will show you the clothes people wore and possibly other details too.

Visit the main library in your area. Here you may find newspapers and magazines that were written in the 1930s. These will provide stories, pictures and advertisements that will give you a detailed idea of life at the time. Your library may keep a map of the 20s or 30s too. This will be very helpful in doing the following:

Explore the streets and buildings of your area. Can you find examples of the big increase in council and private housebuilding? Are these houses built in a certain style? Do newspaper advertisements of the 1930s tell you how much the houses first cost? How much do they cost today? Are there any cinemas left that were in use in the 1930s? Can you find any clues to the presence in your town of the trams that once ran in all the larger towns?

Build up a folder, gathering information and pictures and grouping the material under headings.

Travelling showmen were still quite common in the streets of Britain in the Thirties. This showman has a mobile merry-go-round.

1. Hard Life

The Daily Struggle

Rose Gamble lived in London during the 1930s. Her family, and all her neighbours, struggled hard to provide themselves with home, food and clothes. She remembered that

The great achievement for any family down our street was to have regular wages. After putting by money for the rent, coke, paraffin, we had about sixteen shillings to see us through, so very little was spent on anything but food. Going on a bus was a rare treat and everything else we wanted had to be made out of what we could scrounge.

R. Gamble, *Chelsea Child*

People with jobs had long working days. Helen Forrester lived in Liverpool and remembered when her brother began work.

Alan reached the age of 14 and left school shortly afterwards. I watched him set out for his first job as an office boy in a new suit bought for the occasion from Marks & Spencers. The life of an office boy was very hard. In a tall gloomy building he worked from 8.30 in the morning until 6 o'clock at night and until 1 o'clock on Saturdays for a wage of 7/6 *a week. Office boys were commonly hit when they made mistakes or if they dared to answer back.

H. Forrester, *Liverpool Miss*

An expert who looked carefully at what food, clothes and homes cost decided

These cannot be provided at less than 53/- a week for an urban [*town*] worker with a wife and three children. This allows scarcely any margin, certainly not more than 3/6 a week for holidays, beer and tobacco, visits to a cinema or football match.

B. Seebohm Rowntree, *The Human Needs of Labour*

Many wage earners did not regularly earn 53/-. During the 1930s hundreds of thousands had no work at all. The money paid them by the authorities was far less than 53/-. This money was known as 'the dole'.

1. In what way is the picture a clue to the fact that many workers did not have much money?

This is how a Greenock family of ten people spent their £1 19s 3d a week.

Rent	12/-	Sugar	10d
Gas	3/-	Bread	7/-
Societies (through these money was saved for clothes and doctors' bills)	1/4	Meat	2/10
		Vegetables	11d
		Rice	4d
Coal	2/3	Dripping	3d
Milk	2/4	Tea-bread	6d
Soap	8d	Fish	10d
Potatoes	2/-	Biscuits	4d
Margarine	1/-	Salt and Pepper	1d.
Tea	9d		

(The Pilgrim Trust, *Men Without Work*)

*7/6 is another way of writing 7s 6d
In old money 12d=1s=5p   20s (shillings)=£1

This woman is waking up workers who do not own alarm clocks. She is shooting peas at the bedroom windows. Some 'knockers up' used long poles to tap on windows.

1. *What was a 'rare treat' for Rose Gamble?*
2. *What other 'treats' are mentioned?*
3. *What was the costliest item in the Greenock family's spending?*
4. *What do you think they probably ate a great deal of to keep away hunger?*
5. *List all the clues in the picture on the right that show this is the home of a poor family.*

Homes and Food

Many people lived in slum housing. Families crowded into perhaps just two rooms. Rose Gamble's home, like many others, did not have a bathroom. The lavatory was in a shed in the back yard.

I wouldn't go down to the lav. at night on my own and I kicked up such a fuss one of my elder sisters had to take me. The lav. was a shack in the corner of the yard. [Once] as Lu dragged open the door there was a terrible shriek. I screamed and we fought past each other dropping the candle. 'There's a ghost' sobbed Lu, 'yellin' its 'ead off in the lav.' There was a fearful flopping and squawking noise 'You daft aporths' Mum said 'it's just one of them 'ol chickens'.

Chelsea Child

Feeding the family was the biggest worry. A woman in a Lancashire cotton town whose husband had no work explained

They give us 31/-. You can't feed six on 31/- when you have 8/- to pay in rent. Our eldest

This family are eating their main meal of the day. They are having boiled fish, dry bread and tea.

is working. The other children are at school and thank God they get a meal there. Their breakfast is bread and margarine. Their tea bread and jam. Saturday they get bread and margarine for dinner as well. But on Sunday we manage a meat dinner. In winter we don't dare put anything on the fire after six – we go to bed when we feel cold.

Fenner Brockway, *Hungry England*

Rose Gamble's sister was an expert at finding cheap food.

As there was no refrigeration in any of the shops a lot of food was sold cheaply just before it went off. Luli never missed a quick look into the biscuit boxes, judging the moment when the grocer would put out a fresh box and buying up the broken bits in

5

the old ones. She got cracked eggs and looked around for a twopenny cod's head. Potatoes cost sixpence for seven pounds. A couple of times a week we had to go to a shop where they sold off stale bread, for sixpence you could get at least 3 large loaves.

They bought sixpenny bundles of meat scraps at the butchers. Rose went with a friend, Winnie.

One Friday I put down my sixpence and the butcher whacked an extra large parcel in front of me. Slowly I parted the paper and stared into a wide open eye. 'Its an 'ead,' I cried. 'Win, I've got an 'ead.' 'What sort?' 'Pig's. Its got eyes, an' teeth, an ear 'oles. Everything!'

Chelsea Child

1. What was the main item of food in the home described by Fenner Brockway?
2. When were poor people able to buy food cheaply?

Keeping clean

Mary Charters lived in a little town in Cumberland. She remembered

The house I was brought up in was one up and one down and a kitchen. The lads were locked out on a Saturday night while we were bathed in one of those old fashioned – what you used to wash clothes in. We had a cold water tap. They would put a bucket on the gas ring and boil in that. On washing days [Mother] used to send us to Sarah Jane Thurlow's with a big jug for tupenny broth and then to Phyllis Hogg to get your jug filled with milk for a penny. And that was our dinner when they were washing. They hadn't time to cook. They had to wash in their kitchens with the old-fashioned dolly tubs and poss sticks. And we used to hook [the clothes] on barbed wire and sit and wait till they dried. If you weren't there the cows ate the shirts.

M. Bragg, *Speak for England.*

1. What do you think Mary Charters was bathed in?
2. Why was it not easy to obtain hot water?
3. Why do you think clothes were spread over fence wire and not pegged out on garden lines?

Local Shops

1. People in working class homes did not have refrigerators. What foods would they have to buy very frequently so that they would be fresh?

Shops in working class areas were open for long hours so that people could visit them on their way to work or in the evening, when they came home. Shops had to stock food that people with little money could afford. Joseph Johnson worked in a baker's in Cumberland.

We were a penny for a teacake and threepence for a white loaf. Well, people lived on plain food then. There wasn't so much cake wanted, people hadn't the money. Butter was put onto slates. Big blue slates, to keep cool.

Speak for England

Rose Gamble loved to look in the local sweet shop.

The floor of the window was layered with rows of grubby dishes filled with tiger nuts that tasted like the insides of dusty cupboards, gritty spearmint toffee, aniseed balls, sherbert dabs and sun-faded jelly babies, all at a ha'penny an ounce. The quality stuff was in tall glass jars up on the shelves, but we never paid any attention to them.

Chelsea Child

Quite a number of things could be bought from carts that were pushed, or drawn by animals round the streets. Rose Gamble's nearest dairy

employed a nippy little man who pushed a cart round the streets and sold milk from a churn with a yellow brass lid. People took their jugs out to him and he dipped a measure into the churn on a long milky handle.

On Mondays one of the busiest shops was the pawnbroker's. Ernest Hush was a pawnbroker in Middlesbrough.

People had no, repeat *no* money in their possession on Monday morning. They came to pawn their possessions at 5.0 am to enable them to buy food for breakfast. I came to understand the state of always being hard up and accepting living from hand to mouth as a normal way of life.

K. Hudson, *Pawnbroking*

A group of people who studied poor people in Liverpool decided

In Liverpool two out of three unemployed families admit to having goods in pawn; in some cases as soon as the clothes are bought through a clothing club they go into a pawnshop.

Pilgrim Trust

1. *Why were shops open such long hours?*
2. *Why did they have to sell small quantities of food?*

Assignments

1. *From what you have read here make up the menus for three meals on an ordinary day.*
2. *Imagine you have been asked to join the family in the photograph on page 5 for tea. Describe what you had to eat, what you ate and drank from, how the table was decorated and the food served.*
3. *Design and draw a poster to encourage people to come to your shop.*
4. *What do you think the two women waiting for the pawnshop to open would talk about? Make up a conversation between them in which they explain why they need money and what they are going to pawn.*

Women waiting on a Monday morning for their local pawnshop to open. Notice the shop sign. This pawnbroker's was in London's East End. The broker lent money in return for goods the customers brought in. When customers came back for their goods they paid an extra charge.

2. The Unemployed

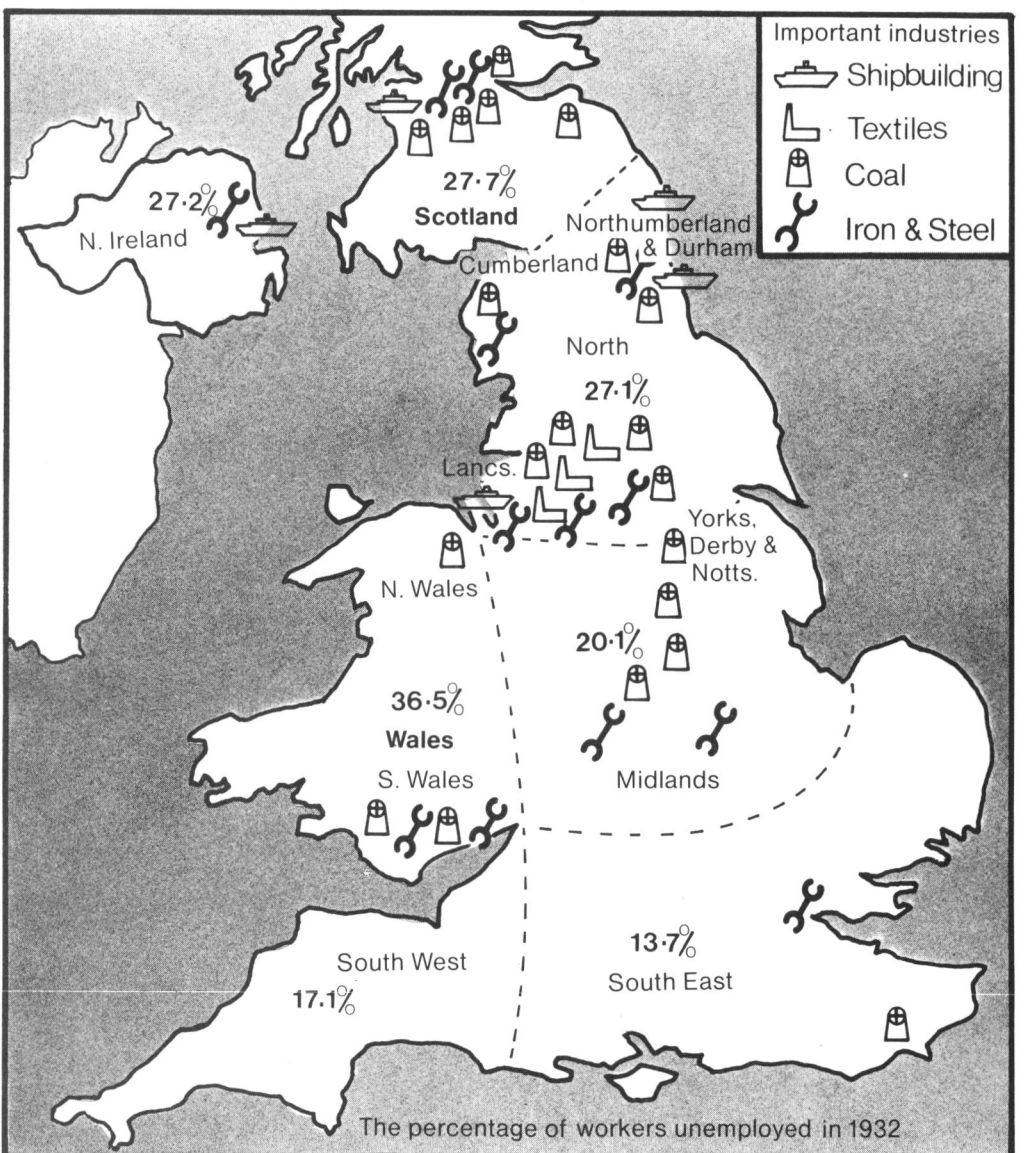

The percentage of workers unemployed in 1932

Legend on map:

Important industries
- Shipbuilding
- Textiles
- Coal
- Iron & Steel

Map labels:
- N. Ireland 27·2%
- Scotland 27·7%
- Northumberland & Durham
- Cumberland
- North 27·1%
- Lancs.
- Yorks, Derby & Notts.
- N. Wales
- Wales 36·5%
- S. Wales
- Midlands 20·1%
- South West 17·1%
- South East 13·7%

The Problem
The number of workers registered out of work

1930	1 917 000	1935	2 036 000
1931	2 630 000	1936	1 755 000
1932	2 745 000	1937	1 484 000
1933	2 521 000	1938	1 791 000
1934	2 159 000	1939	1 514 000

1. *Which part of Britain suffered most from unemployment?*
2. *Which part of Britain suffered least from unemployment?*
3. *In which year were there most unemployed people?*
4. *Which industries were in trouble and not able to provide jobs for all their workers?*

During the 1930s a writer, J. B. Priestley, travelled round England. He noticed

There is the industrial England of coal, iron, steel, cotton, wool, railways; thousands of rows of little houses all alike, mills, warehouses, slag heaps, dock roads, sooty dismal little towns and still sootier grim fortress-like cities. This England makes up the larger part of the Midlands and the North.

J. B. Priestley, *English Journey*

A worker in one of Lancashire's cotton towns explained why so many had no work.

The towns which are supplying the home market are keeping their end up. Feeling the pinch, but not desperate. But the towns which have been supplying the export market are almost famine areas. Take Blackburn. In Blackburn there are 60 mills closed down.

F. Brockway, *Hungry England*

British exports had to fight the exports of many other lands. During the Thirties many countries suffered unemployment; they usually tried to help their own people by taxing imports from countries like Britain. Many of Britain's industries were old-fashioned. A Birmingham man who had lost his job thought that the trouble was

countries which had previously been our customers employed British engineers to establish industry for themselves. By the end of the century the USA and Germany had outstripped us and now France has outstripped us as well. Britain [is] losing its trade to other countries. World trade has collapsed.

Hungry England

1. According to Priestley, where were most of England's industries to be found?
2. Give two reasons why so many people found it hard to find work in the Thirties.

Government Action

The Labour Government that was elected in 1929 was ruined by 1931. It could not agree on what to do about the unemployed. A new 'National' Government was chosen. It included men from the Liberal and Conservative Parties as well as a few Labour MPs.

People with no work were not left to starve. Many workers were part of insurance schemes and had built up savings that lasted for a while. George Orwell, a writer who cared greatly about the problems of the poor, wrote

When a man is first unemployed, until his insurance stamps are exhausted, he draws 17/- for a single man, 9/- for his wife, for each child below 14–3/-. When a man's stamps are exhausted he receives – single man 15/-, man and wife 24/-, children between 3/- and 6/- (depending on age).

George Orwell, *'The Road to Wigan Pier'*

But many people were not part of insurance schemes; even for those who were, money was only paid for six months. Until 1934 such people got help locally. After that date the Unemployment Assistance Board was set up to be in charge of the whole country. The money people received was called 'the dole'. The Government introduced a harsh new rule. It was explained by Rene Cutforth who was a young man in the Thirties.

The new government imposed the Means Test. The Means Test meant that an unemployed man who had come to the end of his insurance was now at the mercy of an [official] empowered to enquire into every halfpenny that found its way into his house,

Ramsay MacDonald had been Labour's leader. In 1931 he became head of the National Government. He is leading his fellow ministers into the back garden of No. 10 Downing Street. The Labour Party expelled him.

The National Unemployed Workers Movement was very active in the Thirties. Its leader was a Communist, Wal Hannington. In 1932 marchers came to London from all over Britain to protest about the Means Test.

if one of the children helped with a milk round or ran errands or even was spotted wearing a new coat, the dole was adjusted accordingly.

R. Cutforth, *Later Than We Thought*

Terry Walsh was a boy in London in the Thirties. His out-of-work father

got about a pound a week from the Public Assistance. But before you were allowed even that you had to get rid of any decent stuff in the house. Half the furniture went before we got a penny.

J. Seabrook, *Working Class Childhood*

George Orwell saw that the unemployed hated the Means Test.

It breaks up families. An old age pensioner would normally live with one of his children: his weekly ten shillings goes towards the household expenses. Under the Means Test he counts as a lodger and if he stays at home his children's dole will be docked. So, perhaps at 70 years of age, he has to turn out into lodgings.

The Road to Wigan Pier

1. *From what you have read here, what harm did the Means Test do?*
2. *Try and suggest one reason that might have been put forward by someone in favour of the Means Test.*
3. *Depending only on its insurance money, how far short would a family of five be from what Rowntree said they would need? (53/- a week).*

Protest!

Many unemployed protested about the way they were treated. They organised marches to London to try and persuade the Government that the dole should be increased and the Means Test abolished.

Stanley Baldwin, who was Prime Minister from 1935 to 1937 complained:

In the opinion of His Majesty's Government such marches can do no good, are liable to cause unnecessary hardship to those taking part in them and are altogether undesirable in this country where every adult has a vote.

The Times, 15.10.1936

The most famous of these marches came from the shipbuilding town of Jarrow in North East England. In 1935 almost threequarters of Jarrow's workers had no job. A local journalist reported that when Palmers, the Jarrow Shipyards closed

It didn't matter if a man was a labourer or a top executive when that lot closed down they were all out of work. And I'm afraid there was little opportunity for them to get work because the rest of Northumberland and Durham were depressed, right through the community from top to bottom it was a staggering blow.

T. Pickard, *Jarrow March*

The people of Jarrow decided to act, as one of them recalled

Well, it was decided that we must do something and the idea of the march . . . not just a collection of men banding themselves together and perhaps going on a hunger march. No, it had to be something different to that. We realised we wanted it to be well organized, something that could be well looked up to.

Jarrow March

Inspector Wright of the Special Branch kept an eye on events. He reported:

On October 5th, 1936, 207 unemployed men of Jarrow with two banners bearing the words

The Jarrow Marchers stop and cook a meal.

'Jarrow Crusade' left that town amidst scenes of great enthusiasm headed by Miss Ellen Wilkinson, MP for Jarrow, carrying a petition for presentation to the House of Commons which was signed by 11,572 people.

Jarrow March

One of the marchers, Sam Rowan, remembered

Our first stop was Chester le Street and we stopped in the field there and our cooks made tea and dished out corned beef sandwiches and the local celebrities came and said they had sleeping accommodation fixed up and that there would be a hot meal.

Jarrow March

In Leicester local shoemakers stayed up all night to mend the marchers' boots. The

11

Many skilled workers had no jobs in the Thirties. This man is making a determined attempt to find work. Has he chosen a time of year when people need plumbers more than usual?

march was widely reported. One London cinema manager sent free tickets so that marchers could see *The Call of the Flesh*! Inspector Wright sent in another report when the Jarrow men reached London.

The marchers were shown round the House of Commons and taken for a trip on the river as far as Tower Bridge and back. It was whilst the men were thus engaged that the Jarrow petition was presented to the House of Commons.

Jarrow March

Parliament turned down the petition for help for Jarrow. The marchers returned sadly home.

1. *Why did Stanley Baldwin think there was no need for marches?*
2. *Why do you think Jarrow men called their march a 'crusade'?*
3. *List all the people who helped the Jarrow marchers.*

Passing the time

Early one Monday morning in the 1930s a young man lay sleeping in his home till . . . .

He awoke at his usual time, dressed and scrambled into the kitchen to gulp down his breakfast. No breakfast was prepared and his mother was still in bed! What had gone wrong? It slowly dawned upon him that there was no need for haste this Monday morning. He was unemployed. After the first shock he trudged wearily back to his room, sat on the edge of his bed and began to think.

The Carnegie Trust, *Disinherited Youth*

1. *What made the man realise there was no need to get up?*
2. *What might he have been thinking as he sat on the edge of the bed?*

In a Welsh mining town, these were common sights . . . .

Men stand aimlessly on street corners. Others work in allotments or on gardens or do carpentry. Some few attend classes, others stroll down the valley. On wet days the Miners' Institute offers papers and a shelter. At nights there are the pictures and the long queues outside the Picture House account for more of the pocket money of the unemployed than do the public houses.

H. Jennings, *Brynmawr*,

George Orwell found a very boring lecture in Sheffield on 'Clean and Dirty Water' was crowded. He was puzzled till one member of the audience told him:

Most of the members are unemployed men who will put up with almost anything in order to have a warm place where they can sit for a few hours.

The Road to Wigan Pier

Other *investigators* reported that

The extent to which the interest and indeed the whole lives of so many of the Liverpool unemployed centre round the [football] pools must be seen to be believed.

The Pilgrim Trust

Some never gave up the search for work and included:

Older men who have not a chance of working again yet make it a practice to stand every morning at 6.0 o'clock at the work gates in the hope that perhaps they may catch the foreman's eye. We had instances of men who had bicycled all over Lancashire and Yorkshire in the hopes of finding something.

The Pilgrim Trust

1. How many different ways of filling up time can you find in this section? Make a list of as many as possible.
2. Why do you think that going to the cinema and filling in the football pools were both so popular?

Assignments

1. What do you think it would have been like on the Jarrow march? Write a letter home from London, as if you were a marcher. Mention your clothes, your food, how you tried to keep your spirits up, how people treated you along the way and what happened in London.
2. Pretend you are an unemployed person in 1934. You are being interviewed on the radio about what life is like since you lost your job. Write down what you would say. Try to give as much information as possible.

Unemployed men passing time in their local public library. The library provided warmth and shelter as well as something to do.

13

3. A Better Life

During the 1930s most people with steady jobs found they were able to afford an increasingly comfortable life. Look carefully at the following list of figures.

(a) In 1914 most working class families had to spend 60 % of all they earned on food and 16 % on rent.
(b) By 1937 most working class families had to spend 35 % of all they earned on food and 9 % on rent.
(c) In 1934 in Coventry and Oxford only 5 % of all insured workers were unemployed.
(d) During the 1930s two million houses were built for sale.
(e) Between 1925 and 1939 the amount of electricity used in Britain increased fourfold.
(f) By 1939 a steady wage bought 15 % more of life's necessities than in 1930.

1. *How much did a family with £3 a week spend each week on food and rent in 1914 and 1937?*
2. *How much extra, out of £3, did a 1937 family have to spend on other things?*
3. *Which part of Britain does not seem to have suffered much from unemployment?*
4. *Name two of the ways in which many people who were better off spent their extra money.*

As J. B. Priestley travelled round England in 1933 he saw many signs of

the new post-war England. This is the England of by-pass roads, of filling stations and factories that look like exhibition buildings, of giant cinemas and dance halls and cafes, bungalows with tiny garages, cocktail bars, Woolworths, motor coaches, wireless, factory girls looking like actresses.

J. B. Priestley, *English Journey*

George Orwell wrote that

Nearly all citizens now enjoy the use of good roads, germ-free water, free libraries. Public education has improved. To an increasing extent the rich and the poor read the same books, see the same films and listen to the same radio programmes. And the differences in their way of life have been diminished by the mass production of cheap clothes and improvements in housing.

G. Orwell, *The Lion and the Unicorn*

Inside a London grocer's, 1937. The shop is lit by an oil lamp and candles because of a power failure. Look at the goods on sale. How similar are they to the goods in your local grocer's?

1. What changes were noticed by both writers?

'New' Industries

J. B. Priestley came from Yorkshire. He was used to seeing huge textile mills. Many of the factories he saw in the South East were quite different, being

decorative little buildings, all glass and concrete and chromium plate, they are evidence that the new industries have moved south. Potato crisps, scent, toothpaste, bathing costumes, fire extinguishers; those are the concerns behind these pleasing facades.

He visited one of these new factories, at Bristol. It was full of

the most ingenious machines in almost every department. One of them has only to be fed regularly with cut tobacco, mile long reels of paper, printing ink and paste to turn out cigarettes by the million. Girls perform most of the tasks, this great factory is a warren of girls in green, pink, brown, blue overalls.

English Journey

Industries that did well made things mainly for the home market, not for export. Many of these industries were to be found in the Midlands and the South of England. They used modern machines. Factories making cars and lorries or electrical goods for the home, provided more and more work in the

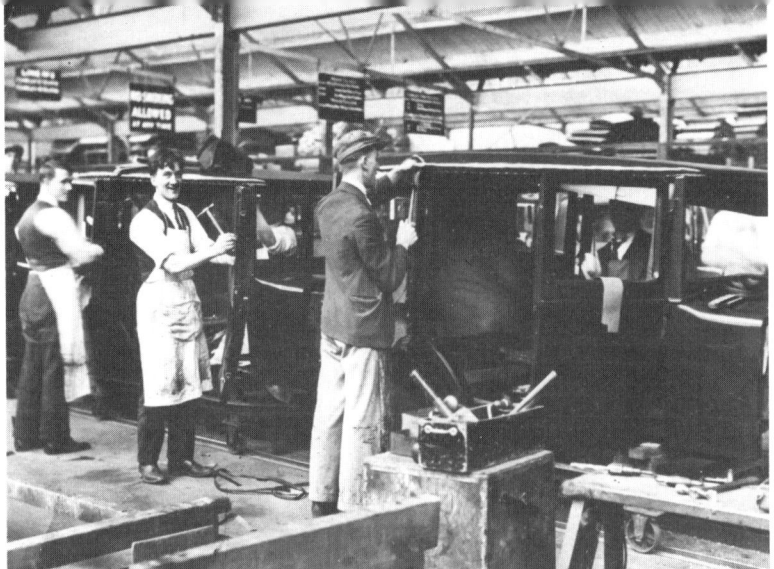

Thirties. J. B. Priestley met a bus-passenger (whilst travelling to Southampton) who thought he could see how to make money. He asked

'What do you think of electric light fittings?' I told him that I knew nothing about them. 'Friend of mine swears by them. All this electricity they're putting in, d'you see. Villages all over, they're getting electric light. I'm going to look into that. Run wireless too as a sideline . . . if I could find a good shop in a growing good-class neighbourhood.

In 1920 there had been only 730 000 electricity consumers in Britain. By 1939 there were nine million. The Central Electricity Generating Board (1926) had covered Britain with its national grid of electric power lines.

These workers are fitting upholstery and decorative trim to Morris cars in Cowley, Oxford. The factory was created by William Morris. Between 1920 and 1938 the number of jobs in car factories more than doubled.

15

Giant pylons carried electricity across Britain. This one has been placed in the gardens of recently-built houses. Many of the new houses built in the Thirties were semi-detached ones.

1. List two sorts of industry that did well in the Thirties.
2. Give one reason why these industries did so much better than industries mentioned in chapter 2.
3. What sort of things would people start buying once they had electricity in the home?

Better Homes

Between 1919 and 1939, 4.3 million new homes were built and many old slum houses were knocked down. The new homes had bathrooms and proper kitchens. George Orwell saw

the Corporation building estates with their row upon row of little red houses are a regular feature of the outskirts of the industrial towns.

G. Orwell, *The Road to Wigan Pier*

Not everyone was keen to move to a better home. Rose Gamble listened to neightbours chatting. They were going to have to leave their slum for a new block of flats.

'There's rules in the buildings.' Mr. Dandy was determined to stir the old girls up.
'What jer mean, rules?' asked Reen's mum.
'No knees up after ten o'clock for a start', he began to count on his fingers.
'No wallpaper, no kids playin' in the yard after dark, no 'ammerin' nails in no walls, no pets nor animals.

'The rents', said Reen's mum 'is going to be something terrible.'
'Yeh, but they got baths ain't they,' put in Mrs. Brimmer.
'What difference does that make?' Mrs. Bellen raised her eyes with contempt.
'Honest', she said, 'can you credit some people! We 'aven't 'ad a bath these thirty years an' never missed it.'

R. Gamble, *Chelsea Child*

The rent for these flats was 16/6 a week.

1. From what you have read in chapters 1 & 2, would the rent of 16/6 be a lot of money for an ordinary family?
2. What would Rose Gamble's neighbours miss when they moved to the new flats?

Many people bought their own homes during the Thirties. Houses were quite cheap and money could be borrowed very easily. Many semi-detached, three-bedroomed houses were around £500.

During the Thirties housework became easier for women who could afford new electric cookers, irons, cleaners and washers.

Many middle-class families had servants to work for them. There were still plenty of women ready to work from early in the morning to late at night six or seven days a week. Naomi Mitchison was a young woman in the Thirties who found servants made life very easy for her.

People could get by quite comfortably on

£600 to £700 a year. Servants' wages went up slowly or were static. A cook could earn about a pound a week. Babies' nappies were only just coming in late in the Thirties. No fridge, no dishwasher, no electric liquidiser, no detergents and no drip dry or spin dryers. Lux Flakes started in the Thirties and by then we had an electric iron. The only mending I ever did myself was sometimes to have a go at a pile of socks. The parlourmaid waited at table, cleared plates, brought the coffee tray through to the drawing room where they had drawn the curtains, perhaps lighted a fire. Above all they washed up. One would find a hot water bottle in one's bed and in the morning a call with orange juice or tea. Breakfast would be there with letters and newspapers on the table.

N. Mitchison, *You May Well Ask*

1. *What sort of tasks at home were harder work in the Thirties than they are today?*
2. *Why do you think many women were willing to work as domestic servants?*

Shopping

During the Thirties shopping became easier and cheaper; shops offered far more goods for sale than ever before. George Orwell did not care for the many new ways in which food was presented.

Thanks to tinned food, cold storage, synthetic flavouring matters, the palate is almost a dead organ. Look at the factory-made foil-wrapped cheese, look at the hideous rows of tins, look at a sixpenny Swiss roll or a twopenny ice-cream. Wherever you look you will see the same slick machine-made article.

The Road to Wigan Pier

But housewives were probably glad that there were tinned fruits, vegetables and meats. They could buy cheap frozen meat from the other side of the world; they had the American cereal 'corn flakes' and porridge that could be made in a few minutes. Food was cheap – and prices went down in the Thirties.

Rene Cutforth remembered

The office worker could have a three-course lunch for a shilling and if he liked to spend 1/3 one of the courses could be steak and onions with chips. There was a Woolworth's in every High Street where everything cost sixpence or less. A kettle, for instance, cost sixpence – and its lid sixpence. Montague Burton, the 'Tailor of Taste', could fit you out with a suit for fifty shillings. It would have a waistcoat; trousers were kept up by a pair of braces. If you were under fifty you opted for a Fair Isle pullover. Shirts were white. Most of the male population still wore the old clinging 'Long Johns' under their trousers.

R. Cutforth, *Later Than We Thought*

A child with pocket money had a huge range

A new electric washing machine.

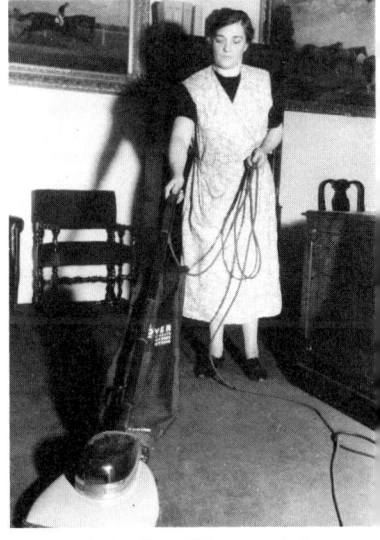

One of the first 'Hoovers'. It was advertised in *Woman's Own* with the words 'Housework is not the drudgery it used to be'.

The new Marks & Spencer's store at Marble Arch, London.

of sweets to choose from. Edward Blishen bought

gobstoppers that changed colour as you sucked, or thick hunks of liquorice, or triangular bags of sherbert with a paddle of toffee to suck and dip with, or cylinders of chocolate shreds, or cough drops, or enormously long strips of very narrow toffee.

E. Blishen, *Sorry Dad*

There were also many old-fashioned shops. In Oxford Penelope Mortimer went to

a dignified shop called Elliston & Cavell, where money and receipts whizzed in lead containers along wires from the counter to the cashier and back again, and there were high chairs for the customers to sit on while they chose their elastic hosiery.

P. Mortimer, *About Time*

Shops like these were usually glad to deliver whatever customers had bought to their homes.

1. Why were there more cheap foods available in the Thirties?
2. What do modern shops use instead of the containers described by Penelope Mortimer?

Assignments

1. From what you have read here, design a notice board for the new buildings near Rose Gamble's telling the people living there about the rules.
2. Design an advertisement to persuade housewives to buy a new electric washing machine you are manufacturing.
3. Imagine you have hired a female servant. Write out a list of her duties, including her getting-up and bed-times.
4. Make up a poster either for Woolworths, or Burtons, that will encourage shoppers to visit your store.
5. Read the following 1932 price list and make up a shopping list that will be as cheap as possible for a family of four for a week.

Flour – 14 lbs	1/8d	Marmalade – 2 lbs	11½d
Rice – 1 lb	3½d	Syrup – 1 lb	6½d
Cornflour – 1 lb	2d	Salt	2d
Custard Powder pack	6d	Eggs each	1d
Tea – ½ lb	1/-	Butter – ½ lb	7d
Coffee – ½ lb	1/2	Cheese – ½ lb	6½d
Sugar – 1 lb	2d	Bacon – 1 lb	1/-
Jam – 1 lb	8d	Carrots each 1b	1½d
Potatoes each 1b	3½d	Turnips each 1b	1½d
Onions each 1b	2d		

What would the same shopping list cost today?

4. A Wealthy Life

In the Thirties Gregory Gladwell lived in a Cumberland village. Near it stood the large home of a wealthy landowner. He remembered

It was there with all the gardens, grooms and maids and food. You have to face it, the Big House was then an asset to the village. It paid us to raise our hats, which is why we did it.

M. Bragg, *Speak for England*

Britain contained wealthy families who were able to live very comfortable lives. Taxes were low and servants were easy to obtain. Rosina Harrison went to work for one of the most famous rich women of the time — Nancy, Lady Astor. The Astors owned several homes. Their main home was Cliveden in Buckinghamshire. It was, 'Rose' Harrison wrote,

composed of a central block with East and West wings. On the ground floor there was a huge hall, the long drawing room, the library, the dining room, Lord Astor's study and Lady Astor's boudoir. Above were the main bedrooms, also the nurseries. In the East wing were guest rooms for about forty visitors. In the West wing were the offices and staff bedrooms. The basement contained the kitchens, the servants' hall, the rooms where the visitors' clothes were pressed and cleaned,

the china room and the wine cellar.

R. Harrison, *My Life in Service*

The great house of Cliveden. Many politicians of the day came here. Nancy Astor was the first woman to take a seat as an MP at Westminster.

In the school holidays the Astors and their servants went to one of the family's other homes. Rose recalled

The holiday visits to Tarbet Lodge on the island of Jura and to Rest Harrow at Sandwich meant a great deal of packing for me because we went for weeks at a time. In addition to the luggage we took on those visits there was always a special piece that came with us, a cow which was transported in a truck attached to the end of the train. His Lordship was very particular about the kind of milk the children drank.

1. Explain why many ordinary people behaved very respectfully towards the wealthy.
2. Make a list of all the different sorts of servants that would be needed in a house like Cliveden.

Good Food

The wealthy often held large dinner parties.

When Richard Lowther worked as a servant for the Earl of Carlisle in 1938 at Naworth Castle

We had some marvellous banquets there. The banquet hall would be nearly as big as the Market Hall. Seat about 150. Sir Miles Lawson was there with his six daughters. So the fashion of the day was these bare backs. So I was going along with this tray, all of a sudden there was one of these dachshunds made a dart out between my legs and I fell over and the soup went right down this woman's back. The screams!

M. Bragg, *Speak for England*

These big meals might consist of as many as ten different courses. The cooks had to work hard. Rosina Harrison saw that the Cliveden kitchens were very busy.

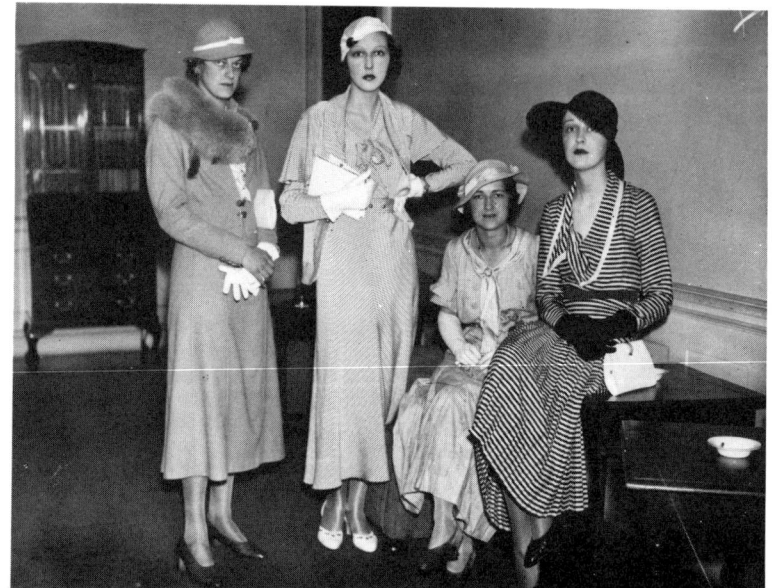

Fashionable clothes of 1933 worn by ladies arranging the very important 'Queen Charlotte's Ball'.

on big party days they were places I kept out of. The kitchens were hives of activity. Some days before Lady Astor would have worked out the menu with the chef. With a dinner party the kitchen is working to almost split second timing. One minute a dish is ready to serve and the next it's past its best. Getting the food from the kitchen to the dining room hot, decorated and ready to serve was the job of the odd-job men.

My Life in Service

At dinner there was once nearly a disaster. A public figure of some standing was talking to Lady Astor as a footman was serving him.

'I need a skivvy for my kitchen, can any of your servants recommend one?'
'What kind of servant do you want?'
'Oh, any little slut will do!'
The footman stepped back and went white as a sheet. Mr. Lee (the butler) told me 'I moved over as quickly as I could and caught his arm just as he was about to pour the hot sauce over the guest's head!'

1. *Why do you think the guest thought it safe to speak so rudely when servants were listening?*
2. *What sort of person would have made a very good 'odd-job' man?*
3. *Write what the butler said to the footman.*

Passing the Time

Wealthy people not only had country homes and London homes, they often owned houses abroad. During the Thirties, holidays in the South of France became fashionable. In Britain the rich passed their time visiting, at dances and banquets, at the theatre and at certain race meetings like Ascot. Rosina Harrison found

Ascot week was really hectic. Every guest room would be occupied. Breakfast was served at 8.30 am and there'd be a dozen hot dishes to choose from. Before this the footmen would have been scurrying along the passages with early morning tea and brass jugs of shaving water. Then downstairs to clean shoes and iron the laces. At around 6 o'clock pm the racing party would return. At 7.45 the gong would sound which was the signal for all the guests to go to their rooms and dress for dinner. The grand finale of Ascot was the Royal Ball at Windsor Castle.

Wealthy women usually had their clothes specially made for them. Rosina Harrison was once astonished to be sent by Lady Astor to buy a dress in Marks & Spencer's.

I found a grey dress with delightful grey pearl buttons. It cost £3.19.6. It fitted her to perfection. She'd come back and tell me her friends had admired it and asked her where she had got it from. 'Did you tell them the truth, my Lady?'
'No, of course not Rose, they'd never have believed me anyway. I told them Jacqmar made it.'

When Richard Lowther worked for the Marquis of Linlithgow he was a valet, responsible for looking after the Marquis' twin boys of 18.

They'd have morning clothes, perhaps three suits, and then they would have various lounge suits for the afternoon. It was a very busy life because they had a clean shirt on every time. Perhaps six shirts each a day.
    First of all you would draw [run] the bath for them. They would have an ordinary morning coat on (for breakfast). They never wore casual clothes like people do now. And then they would go off riding. Then they would come back and change for lunch. During the Court Season there's all these debutante afternoon parties and tea parties. And they were just continually changing all the time. Then of course the big do's in the evening. I think I had 25/- a week. It was a life that buzzed with social events.

Speak for England

1 List all the different ways of passing the time that the wealthy enjoyed.
2. Why do you think Lady Astor was not likely to find one of her friends wearing a Marks & Spencer dress like her own?
3. Do you like the fashionable clothes on page 20? Mention any differences from the clothes of today.

Children

Rosina Harrison described the children of

the family she served.

The Astor children had a traditional upbringing, the nursery, governesses, preparatory and public schools and University. Let me begin with the nursery and Nanny Gibbons. Nanny Gibbons had joined the Astors when Mr. William was born and she lived the rest of her life there. She was devoted to her children, looked after their diet, their clothes and their money. Assisting Nanny Gibbons was a nurserymaid whose job it was to clean the nursery, do the washing and ironing, lay the tables and serve the food, wheel the babies in the pram or, when they were older, take them for walks and play games with them. The big moment of any day for the children when they were little was when they went down from the nursery to join their parents after tea. The boys all went away at the age of eight to their preparatory school.

My Life in Service

1. Children came to see their parents after tea. When do you think they would be sent back to their nursery?
2. Whom do you think a wealthy young child would turn to with problems and secrets?
3. How do you think a wealthy parent would explain why the children spent most of their time with servants and were sent away to school when very young?

Assignments

1. What do you think the boys on the right of the picture below might be saying to each other?
2. Make up an advertisement to be placed in a newspaper for either a Nanny or a Nursemaid. Describe the hours, the duties and the uniform.

(*right*) Two wealthy young Eton schoolboys are being studied by a couple of ordinary boys.

(*left*) Nannies and nursemaids chat in the park.

5. Caring for the sick and the young

Rose Gamble lived in a London slum. The people there were used to serious illnesses.

Diphtheria was not uncommon. We knew two little boys who died of it and a girl in Lu's class lost her younger sister in the same way. 'The Town Hall men', she whispered in a shocked voice, 'baked their rooms out'. Many children got scarlet fever and Mum warned us it was because they played around drainholes. We never had doctor because he charged 3/6 a visit and had to be paid on the dot.

R. Gamble, *Chelsea Child*

1. Why do you think the 'Town Hall men "baked" their rooms'?

About half of Britain's working people belonged to a government scheme. Money was taken from their wages; in return they were able to see a doctor without paying. But the scheme did not cover their families. Nor did it pay for hospital treatment or eye treatment. People had to buy spectacles privately. Many got them in Woolworth's.

Molly Weir lived with her mother in a Glasgow slum. The people there

had great faith in the folk medicine which had been handed down to us. For whooping cough the favourite cure was to suspend the victim over a tar boiler. Mothers would seize unwilling victims and drag them from the house. Some managed to get a card which admitted them to the gasworks and swore by the effectiveness of the fumes there.

One horrible scourge was ringworm. I caught it myself and was hauled off to the doctor. My head was shaved and a bottle of iodine poured over it. Another head invasion almost impossible to avoid was nits and lice. Worms was another affliction. It was quite usual to hear big brothers or sisters asking the chemist for a 'worm powder for my wee sister'

. . . . One neighbour brought her wee boy who had very bad rickets. My mother told me that wee Eck's mother had been too poor to give him real milk when he was an infant and had given him weak tea in his bottle and his bones hadn't developed. I gazed with interest at his wizened little face and at his poor bent legs.

M. Weir, *Best Foot Forward*

1. List serious illnesses common in the Thirties.
2. Which were caused by (a) dirty living conditions, (b) poor diet?
3. Why did most ordinary people rarely visit a doctor?

Even workers who were in the health insurance scheme could not always afford the doctor's treatment. Helen Forrester lived in Liverpool. One day

my parents came home and found me shivering in my bed, they sent for the doctor

A public wash-house in 1934. Thousands of homes did not have hot and cold water supplies. Notice the scrubbing board where dirt was rubbed out of clothes.

with whom I had registered my name. He came marching into the smelly bug-ridden bedroom. He examined me and diagnosed influenza and tonsillitis. He ordered a light diet of milk, eggs and orange juice. Mother did make bread and milk for me and for the rest I had Oxo cubes disolved in hot water, toast and tea.

H. Forrester, *Liverpool Miss*

Hospitals

This is how a woman who lived in a London slum explained how her large family had suffered from illnesses.

I have just had my eighth baby; I have lost three, three of the others have been in hospital for heart trouble and rheumatism. One I paid six shillings a week for at Carshalton, one I paid four shillings per week for at St Stephens; the first baby I lost, we paid six shillings at Fulham Babies Hospital for him.

M. Spring Rice, *Working Class Wives*

Patients waiting for treatment at Gravesend Hospital, 1939.

Some hospitals were originally set up by wealthy people. By the Thirties they tried to keep going by asking patients to pay what they could and by raising money from events like flag days. Other hospitals were run by local authorities. Naomi Mitchison belonged to a family with enough money not to have to worry about doctors' bills. She thought

Hospitals had been greatly improved by the experiences of the 1914–18 war. Surgery, including anaesthetics, had improved out of all knowledge. When Murdoch got diphtheria he had the correct jab and so had the rest of the family. Most ordinary operations were done at home if the home was clean and roomy. The children had their tonsils out at home. It was a case of scrubbing a wooden table, getting a new piece of Mackintosh sheeting – and plenty of confidence.

N. Mitchison, *You May Well Ask*

1. Name the two sorts of hospital found in the Thirties.
2. Why would a war have helped medical treatment?

Better Care

Health care improved in the Thirties. Rose Gamble's school

regularly had visits from the nurse, 'Nitty Nora,' and we queued up to see her in an empty classroom. She parted and lifted our hair with a metal comb which she dipped into a white bottle of disinfectant. Several kids got a card from her and had to go off to the cleansing station.

Chelsea Child

A Blackburn lady explained how helpful the new local clinic had been.

I was married very young at the age of fifteen years, my mother died when I was thirteen so I really had no one to tell me anything. I have two lovely children. I have consulted the clinic when anything has been the matter such as colds and have found them a great help as I think clinics are a fine thing for young mothers and anyone in need of anything such as cough mixture, or powders, also for the Doctor or Nurse's advice.

Working Class Wives

There were improvements in some treatments. An Aberdeen doctor, James Fowler learned from America about

the liver treatment of anaemia. The liver had to be taken raw and the patients had to take $\frac{1}{2}$ to $\frac{3}{4}$ pound per day, it was rather a nauseous mess that appeared in front of the patients. In the Thirties we came to the new preventative medicine, a vaccine was discovered which we used to immunise all the children against diphtheria.

J. Fowler, *Dr. Jimmy*

1. *Why do you think Rose Gamble and her friends chose that nickname for the nurse?*

2. *As well as curing sick people, what else did James Fowler hope to do?*

At school

When Rose Gamble first went to school, she set off cheerfully with her sister:

With one hand I clutched the elbow of her sleeve and in the other I held a brown paper bag with my name written on it. Inside was a thick slice of bread and marge.

There were very few books.

We had no exercise books and received half a sheet of paper for dictation. For arithmetic we worked our sums down the narrow strip of paper. Every moment of time was filled with work. There were no discussions, no pots of paint, no acting. We rarely left our seats except for an hour and a half a week when the girls did country dancing and the boys had team games in the playground.

Chelsea Child

Henry Fell was a pupil in a Cumberland elementary school and remembered

Elementary teaching in those days was the three 'Rs' – reading, writing and arithmetic. I can only remember a quarter of an hour a week being devoted to music lessons. We were for ever spelling, all the class shouting out the spelling. The Headmaster said, 'Henry, I think you should try and go for the scholarship. I think you could pass your

Milk was provided cheaply to school children. it came in 1/3 pint bottles. About 4% of children were so poor they were allowed free school dinners.

examination.' But I wasn't keen to go. If I could get a job when I was fourteen it would be a big help to my mother. I know the scholarship's free but you've got to have better clothes and there's a bit of uniform to buy and there's books and a schoolbag. So I deliberately made some mistakes in my exams.

Speak for England

Henry Fell had made sure he did not go to a grammar school. Most pupils in the grammar schools (to which they went when they were eleven years old) were paid for by their parents. Just a few were allowed in free if they passed a special examination. Edward Blishen passed. He found it was easy to spot which pupils were paid for.

In the paying pupils I saw all the handsome and fascinating snobs and heroes and bounders of the school stories. They wore flannels that did not, like the cheaper trousers worn by scholarship boys, turn yellow and baggy. They had different voices.

E. Blishen, Sorry Dad

1. Why did most children not go to grammar schools?
2. What do you think the 'different voices' of the fee-paying pupils sounded like?

Assignments

1. Imagine you are a parent whose child has whooping cough. Write what you would say to explain to the child how and why you're going to treat it.
2. Make up a poster to be pinned up outside a public wash-house. Explain in it what the wash-house offers and why local people should use it.
3. How do you think a new clinic would have advertised itself? Design a poster that will encourage women to come to the clinic.
4. From what you have read here make up a timetable for a day's lessons in an elementary school.
5. Look at the uniforms pupils are wearing. Make up an advertisement for a shop that sells school uniforms. Include sketches of the clothes.
6. The children in the last picture are having a lesson on 'The Sea Shore'. What do you think was written and drawn on the blackboard?

A fortunate class on an outdoor expedition, 1933.

6. Spare Time

Most parents in the Thirties could not afford expensive toys. A Blackburn man who was a schoolboy at the time remembered

We played out in the street all the time. All our games had their season – marbles, hoops, hopscotch. At that time I think the streets offered a rich and warm background for a child: the women sitting on the doorsteps on sunny afternoons, the excitement of misty autumn evenings when it started to get dark early and you could get away with all sorts of mischief.

J. Seabrook. *Working Class Childhood*

Rose Gamble and her friends enjoyed street games too.

We were lucky to be able to use the street for everything we wanted to do. Every lamp post had a wicket chalked on it and we tied lengths of green-grocer's sisal [string] to the lamp-lighter's bars for swings. On summer evenings it was the long rope skipping season.

R. Gamble. *Chelsea Child*

1. Which games mentioned here are still played today?
2. Why do you think children in the Thirties played in the street far more than children today?

When children grew up they still often gathered in the streets. In the Cumbrian

An ice-cream seller. Street traders were very common in the Thirties.

town of Wigton, Harry Watson recalled

In those days all the farm lads and lasses used to come into the town on a Saturday night and a Sunday night. And they used to walk from Market Hill to the church and back again. There were hundreds of people in the street, just walking. People were in their best. You see there was nothing else to do.

M. Bragg. *Speak for England*

During winter evenings many people read books and magazines. By the Thirties the country's schools had managed to teach most people to read. There were libraries and (from 1935) new paperback 'Penguin' books to be bought for sixpence each. Rene Cutforth thought

It was a great decade for books and writers; besides the normal free libraries there were many others where for from a penny to sixpence you could borrow a book for a fortnight. Boots the Chemists ran a library at most branches and travelling libraries toured the villages.

R. Cutforth, *Later Than We Thought*

Penelope Mortimer had enough money to afford another kind of entertainment.

I preferred popular songs bought on small sixpenny records from Woolworth's. I played them on a red portable gramaphone, 'Tiptoe through the Tulips', 'All by Yourself in the Moonlight'. I would stuff my socks into the loud-speaker in the hope that they (my parents) wouldn't hear it and be angry.

P. Mortimer, *About Time*

During the Thirties it became very fashionable to take vigorous exercise.

A bicycle cost just a few pounds. Trams, buses and trains carried people out of towns so that they could walk in the countryside. But most working men still preferred the public house after a hard day's work. In York there were 156 public houses in 1938. Most were old fashioned, like this one:

Just within the main entrance is the public bar capable of holding, at a pinch, about thirty people, where darts and dominoes are played. There are half a dozen spitoons on the floor, which is covered with sawdust. Down a passage is the smoking room. The seats are upholstered in horse hair.

B. S. Rowntree, *Poverty and Progress*

1. People in the Thirties often wandered about in town centres at weekends; what entertainments might they go to today?
2. What do you notice about a Thirties public house that you would not expect to find in a modern one?

(*left*) A display in 1935 given in Hyde Park by a popular organisation of the Thirties called 'The Women's League of Health and Beauty'.

(*right*) A group of ramblers gathering at Waterloo Station, 1932.

Special Occasions

During the Thirties different sorts of tea rooms and cafes opened which people visited for a treat. Edwin Muir went to an Edinburgh tea-room where a small orchestra entertained the customers.

The players are wearing light flannels with red sashes round their waists. Waitresses in neat dresses bustle about bearing ham and eggs, Welsh rabbits, scones, cakes, fruit salad, lemonade, ginger beer and ice-cream.

E. Muir, *Scottish Journey*

Even the poorest families tried to make Christmas a special occasion. Rose Gamble's father

transformed the mantlepiece into a snow scene with cotton wool. We hung our socks up in a row and I got a little bag of gold-covered chocolate coins and a packet of coloured chalk. We had boiled belly of pork for dinner and huge helpings of currant duff for afters with custard.

On Boxing Day the Gambles went to the pantomime, climbing up to the cheapest seats at the top of the theatre.

The first sight of the gods was a shock, for the steepness of the seating took your breath away. There were no real seats, just curved layers of stone each covered with a strip of thin matting. Immediately below us the upper circle was packed full. People began to clap when the conductor suddenly appeared. The advertisements disappeared upwards. Softly, slowly, the lights dimmed. Like lightning the red curtains flew away.

R. Gamble, *Chelsea Child*

1. How different was Rose Gamble's Christmas from your Christmas today?

The Cinema

By 1930 the 'talkies' had just arrived and the days of the silent film were coming to an end. The cinema became an enormously popular entertainment. By 1937 twenty million people went to the pictures every week.

Many of the films of the time helped people to escape from hard and boring lives. A shop assistant of the time said

Films have influenced me. I've imagined myself in the role of Cowboy, Indian and Badman and as a hero. I've been a little frightened of terror films. I often get lumps in my throat during a sad scene.

J. P. Mayer, *British Cinemas and their Audiences*

The unemployed found the warmth and comfort of cinemas very attractive. When a woman whose husband had no job was asked

Ever get a bit of pleasure?' she replied, 'Yes: once a week we go to the pictures. The three children at twopence each; I have

The interior of one of the new luxury cinemas of the Thirties. This cinema was called the 'Granada'. Many cinemas were given names that were meant to sound impressive.

Football was very popular. The man carrying the FA Cup his team has won is Dixie Dean, one of the most famous forwards of the time.

to pay fivepence. It's a big slice in the week's money but for me it's pictures or going mad. It's the only time I forget my troubles.'

F. Brockway, *Hungry England*

Some small local cinemas were not very comfortable, but many new huge ones were built in the Thirties. The writer J. B. Priestley described how luxurious they seemed to ordinary people. When customers entered

they first walked through an enormous entrance hall illuminated by a huge central candelabra. Footmen in chocolate and gold waved them towards the two great marble balustrades, the wide staircases, the thick carpets into which their feet sank as if they were the feet of archdukes. Several search-lights were focussed on an organ keyboard and the organ itself was shaking out cascades of treacly sound.

J. B. Priestley, *Angel Pavement*

Assignments

1. *Imagine you have been taken out to a cafe for a treat. Write out what you tell a friend afterwards to explain all you saw, heard and ate.*
2. *Using the information in the words and pictures, design a large colourful poster or advertisement for a cinema to make it sound as attractive as possible.*

7. On Holiday

1931	1.5 million people were entitled to paid holidays
1939	11.0 million people were entitled to paid holidays
1930	Youth Hostels Association set up. 1939–400 YHA hostels
1937	Blackpool took in over 7.0 million visitors who stayed there at least one night

1. How many more people enjoyed paid holidays in 1939 compared to 1931?

2. Where did many of them go for their holidays?

Holidays on the coast and in the country were easier to enjoy in the Thirties because of improvements in travel. A huge network of railway lines covered Britain. Steam engines pulled the trains. Penelope Mortimer loved setting off on holiday by train.

I remember the lovely dirty smuts in our eyes, grimy faces, blackened hands. The driver and fireman – wearing a sack on his head to protect him from the heat and flying cinders – were black in face, and their teeth shone; they would talk to you if you felt like making conversation before the train started. My mother always closed the windows before we went into a tunnel and red hot sparks flew by.

P. Mortimer, *About Time*

Cars opened up the countryside to family outings.

Many people who had never owned a car before, bought one in the Thirties. Barbara Wilson, a young lady living in Cumberland, discovered

I had £100 in my account and I was absolutely thrilled because I found that £100 would buy a Morris Minor, funny little things with two seats and they had a canvas hood you used to fold back when it was a nice day. Of course you didn't have to do a test or anything in those days. You just drove.

M. Bragg, *Speak for England*

Until 1930 cars were limited to travelling at 20 mph. In that year the limit was abolished. Many accidents followed and in 1934 a new law was passed. 30 mph was the fastest anyone could travel in areas where there were many houses. An angry Member of Parliament complained

It is true 7000 people are killed in motor accidents but people are getting used to the new conditions. No doubt many of the older Members will recollect the numbers of chickens we killed in the early days. We used to come back with the radiator stuffed with feathers. It was the same with dogs. Dogs get out of the way of motor cars nowadays and you never kill one. These things will right themselves.

N. Branson and M. Heinemann, *The Thirties*

1. *Why was travelling by train in the Thirties likely to make people dirty?*
2. *What did the MP think would happen to the road accident figures soon?*

At the Seaside

Molly Weir's mother had very little money, yet she managed to save up for little holidays.

On one holiday when my mother had managed to accumulate a rare healthy dividend from the Co-operative, she had the fanciful notion of taking rooms 'with attendance'. She told us impressively that it meant that we would just have to do the shopping and the cooking ourselves and the landlady would keep the rooms clean and clear the table and do the dishes for us.

Best Foot Forward

the seaside. Many of them used this 'apartment' method. In many boarding houses the landladies cooked the food the visitors had bought and charged extra for providing pepper and salt and sauce. Eleanor Schofield enjoyed her Blackpool boarding house holidays:

We used to do our own buying-in when we got there and each day we would go and buy our own meat or fish for the day and Mrs. Cavanagh did all the cooking. We went each year, we still went after we were married and it cost us 28/- per week for a double bed and all the cooking. My husband was the only chap she would give a pint pot of tea to, all the others had to have cups.

J. K. Walton, *The Blackpool Landlady*

1. *What were the main differences between Molly Weir's apartments and Eleanor Schofield's?*
2. *Why do you think Mrs. Cavanagh gave Eleanor Schofield's husband a special pot of tea?*

Assignments

1. *Write a reply to the MP's speech about car accidents.*
2. *Design an advertisement for the £100 Morris Minor car.*
3. *Design an advertisement for a Blackpool boarding house.*

Most people who managed a holiday went to

8. In the News

Newspapers and magazines

During the 1930s Britain's newspapers tried hard to win bigger sales. They started to make their pages more attractive, they used more pictures and bigger headlines. Some of them paid men to go to people's homes to try and persuade them to buy their newspapers.

Some papers offered generous gifts to new customers. Others entertained their readers with gossip about the lives of film stars, descriptions of how the Loch Ness Monster had been sighted and attempts to get readers to share their thoughts by writing in to the newspaper. The *Daily Mirror* printed this invitation

'If only I could tell'
These words are often on the lips of every husband and wife. 'If only I could tell him about the irritating habit of his that drives me mad'.

Well here's the chance to open your heart and tell the truth. Don't bottle it up any more. Tell the Mirror. Address to 'Secrets'. Names and addresses will not be published.'

H. Cudlipp, *Publish and be Damned*

1. From what you have read in earlier chapters can you suggest why more people bought newspapers and magazines in the Thirties?

2. Mention four methods tried by the newspapers to win more readers.

The Radio

Many families enjoyed a new source of news and entertainment.

The BBC had been set up in 1926. The new radio programmes were strictly run by Sir John Reith. He would not allow programmes to begin on Sundays until after 12.30 pm so that people could go to church. The news, plays, stories and music that poured out from the radio made a great difference to people's lives. George Orwell thought that it was a change for the worse, writing

There are now millions of people to whom the blaring of a radio is a more normal background to their thoughts than the song of birds.

G. Orwell, *The Road to Wigan Pier*

1. Explain in your own words why George Orwell was against radios.
2. If you had lived in the Thirties would you have agreed with him? Give a reason for your answer.

Exciting News

There were plenty of stories in the Thirties with which newspapers and the radio entertained people.

The story of Amy Johnson was especially

A radio, or wireless, from the 1930s.

Amy Johnson preparing for her solo flight to Australia, 1930.
Notice the name painted on her green aircraft and the spare propellor.

Sir Malcolm Campbell standing by his racing car *Bluebird*. His son Donald is sitting in the car. In 1935 Campbell captured the world land speed record in *Bluebird*. He travelled over the Bonneville Flats, Utah, USA, at 30,113 mph.

popular. She was, Rene Cutforth remembered,

a pretty girl brought up in Hull where her father owned a fish business. She was a typist but had made herself a fully qualified pilot and mechanic. Amy bought an old green Gipsy Moth, called it 'Jason', re-built it and flew single-handed to Australia in it in 1930.

R. Cutforth, *Later Than We Thought*

Amy then married a pilot and continued flying. She died in the Second World War while flying a transport plane.

1. *Do you think there would be many women pilots in 1930?*
2. *Why does Amy Johnson have a special place in flying history?*

People in the Thirties were very interested in speedy travel. Records for travelling quickly by land, sea and air were broken again and again. Older ways of travelling declined.

People also enjoyed reading about sport. The England cricket team's Australian tour of 1932–3 led to many newspaper stories. W. H. Ferguson travelled with the English team to look after the luggage. He reported

Douglas Jardine, as tour captain, decided that his one chance of dislodging such supreme Australian batting artists as Bradman lay in leg theory bowling. Larwood, the fastest bowler in the world, was accurate enough to be able to send his deliveries down the leg side ball after ball. I watched distinguished cricketers using their bats as a not-so-bold knight might have used his shield, the Australian dressing room resembled a casualty clearing station. There followed a cable from the Australian Cricket Board 'Bodyline bowling is unsportsmanlike. Unless it is stopped at once it is likely to upset the friendly relations existing between Australia and England.'

Jardine's team beat the Australians. *The Times* newspaper said

There is nothing new in the kind of bowling to which exception is now being taken. English players some years ago suffered many a shrewd knock. Australians know that cricket is not played with a soft ball.

The Times 19.1.1933

1. *Do you think Larwood's bowling against the Australians was 'sporting'?*

The Abdication Story

In January 1936 King George V died. His popular oldest son became King Edward VIII. Until now, Rene Cutforth wrote,

His role in life had been Prince Charming. He had been seen dancing in night clubs, went around with girls a good deal and had broken his collarbone while foxhunting.

Though forty years old he had retained a remarkably youthful appearance. He proposed to marry Mrs. Wallis Simpson, an American who had divorced one husband and was now divorcing another. The British Press printed nothing on the subject but on the Continent and in the USA it was the biggest newspaper scandal of the century.

Later Than We Thought

Stanley Baldwin, the Prime Minister, and the rest of Britain's leaders opposed the King's marriage. They persuaded the King to abdicate since he insisted on marrying Mrs. Simpson.

Edward became Duke of Windsor. George, his younger brother, became King *instead*.

1. *Do you think Edward VIII should have given up his throne? Give reasons for your answer.*
2. (a) *Give at least two reasons why people at the time might have been sorry to see King Edward abdicate.*
   (b) *What reasons might have made Stanley Baldwin oppose the King's marriage?*

Assignments

1. *Make up a* **Daily Mirror** *'Secrets' page in which several people have sent in their grumbles.*
2. *Imagine you are a newspaper reporter. Write a short report describing Amy Johnson's plane, what she plans to do and the dangers that face her. Head it 'Croydon, 5th May 1930'. (This was when Amy set off.)*

Edward, now Duke of Windsor, married Mrs Simpson in 1937.

9. Fascists

Fascists in Europe

During the 1930s Europe was troubled by fears of war and by actual fighting in Spain. Many people felt these troubles were caused by the Fascist leaders of Italy and Germany. Benito Mussolini became Italy's leader in 1922. Adolf Hitler was elected to power in Germany in 1933. Both men built up the strength of their armed forces. Both tried to increase their countries' power by capturing more land. Hitler, especially, ruled his country very harshly. He blamed Germany's troubles on the many Jewish people who lived there peacefully.

Penelope Mortimer visited Vienna in Austria, which Hitler had captured for Germany in 1938.

Hitler and Mussolini taking the salute at a parade. Mussolini's Fascists borrowed this kind of salute from the times of the Roman Empire, and Fascists in other lands copied them.

A parade of Nazi banners at Nuremberg in 1933. The men carrying the banners are Brownshirts', members of Hitler's private army, the S.A.

One April evening we walked over to the Jewish district. Men and women stood outside their shops holding placards 'Do not buy from Jewish pigs'. The S.A. lolled about, they looked in disgust at the victims. A girl of about sixteen was made to kneel on the pavement, stand up, kneel, stand up, kneel.

P. Mortimer, *About Time*

The Nazis began to put Jews in special concentration camps. There they treated them very brutally and finally murdered several million of them. Some Jews escaped from Germany to other countries. Rose Gamble noticed, in 1938,

Quite suddenly in the middle of the term new girls came to the school. They spoke hardly any English and we soon discovered that they were Jewish refugees from Germany. On the newsreels I watched Hitler making speeches to thousands of people and I saw rows of soldiers in steel helmets. In the newspapers there were photographs of shabby old men cleaning the gutters in German streets and they wore marks on their clothes to show that they were Jews.

R. Gamble, *Chelsea Child*

1. Why do you think the Jews in Germany could not do much about Hitler's treatment of them?
2. If you had been a Jew living in Vienna in 1938, what would you have tried to do?

Fascists in Britain

Jewish people who escaped to Britain found that here too there was a Fascist Party. Its leader was Oswald Mosley. He was a wealthy man who had been a Minister in a Labour Government. But he decided ordinary political parties could not solve Britain's troubles and that what the country needed was a great and powerful leader – himself. He set up the British Union of Fascists [BUF] in 1932. He wrote to his followers:

Our object is no less than the winning of power for Fascism, which we believe is the only salvation for our country. We are now organising constant propaganda meetings and route marches through our great cities. We need your help. Will you give it?

C. Cross, *The Fascists in Britain*

1. What did Oswald Mosley think was needed to improve life in Britain?
2. Who do you think might have supported him?
3. Why do you think Mosley (like Hitler) was so fond of having a great many flags at his meetings?

The BUF wore black uniforms.
In 1934 a writer, Vera Brittain, went to the biggest of all BUF meetings. It was held in Olympia. She reported:

The 'leader' appeared, preceded by a fanfare of trumpets and a Blackshirt procession. The band played a German march; the beams from the arc lamps focused on the platform and Sir Oswald strained to speak. Interruptions burst from a gallery: Blackshirts leaped over chairs and a noisy scrimmage began. Sir Oswald raised his voice, 'You can see how badly a Blackshirt force is needed to defend free speech in Britain'. Opposite us a man cried 'Does Hitler stand for free speech?' A group of Blackshirts promptly knocked him down and pummelled him. The interrupter was frog-marched from the hall.

V. Brittain, *Testament of Experience*

The meeting broke up with a great deal of fighting. Several MPs complained about the brutal behaviour of Blackshirts. But the BUF was never large. At its Peak it had around 15 000 members. In 1937 it tried to stir up trouble in London with a march. Over 6000 police gathered to protect the 3000 Fascists from huge crowds. Afterwards marches and private uniforms were banned.

1. How did Mosley try to make himself seem important at the meeting?

Assignments

1. What do you think a German Jewish girl might have said to Rose Gamble about why she came to Britain? Write what she said. Mention Hitler, his brownshirts and their meetings, and how she and her family were treated.
2. How would a meeting like the one described be advertised? Design a poster for it.

Oswald Mosley, leader of British Fascists, at a meeting held in 1934 at Olympia, London.

10. The End of the Thirties

Chamberlain before going into discussions with Hitler at Munich, 1938.

During the later Thirties Britain prepared for war. The leaders of Britain's armed forces were very worried. In 1937 they declared

We are in a position of having threats at both ends of the Empire from strong military powers, that is Germany and Japan, while in the centre we have lost our security in the Mediterranean.

Annual Review of the Chiefs of Staff, H.M.S.O.

The greatest danger came from Hitler's Germany. The German airforce was powerful and could easily reach Britain. Germany had taken over Austria and was demanding a part of Czechoslovakia. Britain's Prime Minister (1937–40) was Neville Chamberlain. He feared that a war between Germany and Czechoslovakia would drag much of Europe into a terrible conflict. He said

How horrible, fantastic, incredible it is that we should be digging trenches and trying on gas masks here because of a quarrel in a far away country between people of whom we know nothing.

A. Calder, *The People's War*

1. From what you have seen and read in this section try and work out what sort of war the British feared they were going to suffer.

Munich

Chamberlain decided to try and prevent war by going to meet Hitler in September 1938 at Munich. There Britain and France agreed to let Germany take a large and important slice of Czechoslovakia. He returned home to cheering. *The Times* newspaper declared

No conqueror returning from a victory on the battlefield has come home adorned with nobler laurels than Mr. Chamberlain from Munich yesterday.

The Times, 1.10.38

Not everybody agreed. Winston Churchill, one of Britain's leading MPs, told the House of Commons,

The German dictator, instead of snatching his victuals [food] from the table, has been content to have them served to him course by course. I believe the Czechs, left to themselves and told they were going to get no help from the Western Powers, would have been able to make better terms than they have got – and they could hardly have worse.

Virginia Cowles remembered how feeling in Britain changed. At first

Peace was the important thing. Once more

the music was playing and Mr. Chamberlain was the hero of the day. Business firms advertised their gratitude in the newspapers; shops displayed Chamberlain dolls and sugar umbrellas; and in Scandinavia there was a movement to present the British leader with a trout stream. Only a few people shook sad heads and stared gloomily into the future.

On March 15th, 1939, Hitler's troops marched into Prague [Czechoslovakia's capital]. That date will go down in history as the date England woke up. Sugar umbrellas disappeared from shop windows. From then on the nation prepared for war.

V. Cowles, *Looking for Trouble*

1. *Why did many people cheer Chamberlain after Munich?*
2. *Why did some people not share in this support for Chamberlain?*
3. *What made most people change their minds and decide that war was likely?*

The Coming of War

Hitler now demanded part of Poland. Britain and France declared they would support Poland. A war now seemed so probable that children in cities likely to be bombed were sent away to safer places.

Then, on 1 September 1939, the Germans attacked Poland. This is how the news reached workers in a cotton mill. It was

Through a woman hairdresser in Derby Street coming into the mill to tell the manager who told an oiler and greaser who came round telling various weavers. Some believed the news, some didn't. Then one or two went out of the mill and bought a special [newspaper]. Then they all believed it. One weaver had hysterics. She had a son. A few were crying, but on the whole they didn't bother much till about four o'clock when the boys got their call-up papers at the mill. At four o'clock they were all working. At five they were in uniform waiting for their pay. The oldest was only 24. They were all given a hearty send off. They had a mixture of bravado and fear on their faces.

J. Lehmann, *I Am My Brother*

The Thirties ended with Britain at war. It was the war that finally ended the problem of unemployment. Everyone was needed to fight in the war, or work at home.

1. *Why did Britain finally declare war on Germany?*
2. *Describe how the young soldiers were feeling as they left home to go to war.*

Assignments

1. *Imagine you are a shopkeeper who is pleased with with the news from Munich. Design a poster to put in your shop window.*
2. *In this book you have read a great deal about the Thirties. Is there anything about that time that would have made you enjoy living then?*

Children being taken out of London to escape the expected air-raids, August, 1939. They are wearing labels with their names on and carrying gas masks.

Further Reading

General Reading

N. Branson & M. Heinemann, *Britain in the 1930s*, Weidenfeld & Nicolson, 1971

R. Cutforth, *Later Than We Thought*, David & Charles, 1976

A. Delgado, *Have You Forgotten Yet?* David & Charles, 1973

R. Graves & A. Hodge, *The Long Weekend*, Faber & Faber, 1940

J. Laver, *Between the Wars*, Vista Books, 1961

C.L. Mowat, *Britain Between the Wars*, Methuen, 1955

M. Muggeridge, *The Thirties*, Collins, 1971

J. Stevenson & C. Cook, *The Slump*, Jonathan Cape 1977

J. Stevenson, *Social Conditions Between the Wars*, Penguin, 1977

Picture Collections

J. Symons, *The Angry Thirties*, Eyre Methuen, 1976

J. Symons, *Between the Wars*, Batsford, 1972

Recollections and Documents

Annual Review of the Chief of Staff, HMSO, 1937

H.L. Beales & R.S. Lambert, *Memoirs of the Unemployed*, *Listener Magazine*, 1934

R. Blythe, *Akenfield*, Allen Lane, 1969

M. Bragg, *Speak for England*, Secker & Warburg, 1976

V. Brittain, *Testament of Experience*, Victor Gollancz, 1957

A. Fenner Brockway, *Hungry England*, Victor Gollancz, 1932

A. Calder, *The People's War*, Jonathan Cape, 1969

V. Cowles, *Looking for Trouble*, Hamish Hamilton, 1941

C. Cross, *The Fascists in Britain*, Barrie & Rockcliffe, 1961

K. Feiling, *Life of Neville Chamberlain*, Macmillan, 1946

W.H. Ferguson, *My Cricket, the Autobiography of W.H. Ferguson*, as told to David R. Jack, Nicholas Kaye, 1957

H. Forrester, *Liverpool Miss*, 1939

R. Gamble, *Chelsea Child*, BBC/Ariel Books, 1979

R. Harrison, *Rose, My Life in Service*, Cassell, 1975

K. Hudson, *Pawnbroking*, Bodley Head, 1982

J. Lehmann, *I am my Brother*, Longman, 1960

H. Macmillan, *Winds of Change*, Macmillan, 1966

J.P. Mayer, *British Cinemas and their Audiences*, Dennis Dobson, 1948

N. Mitchison, *You May Well Ask*, Gollancz, 1979

P. Mortimer, *About Time*, Penguin, 1979

E. Muir, *Scottish Journey*, Heinemann, 1933

G. Orwell, *The Lion and the Unicorn*, Secker & Warburg, 1941 and *The Road to Wigan Pier*, Victor Gollancz, 1937

T. Pickard, *Jarrow March*, Allison & Busby, 1982

Pilgrim Trust, *Men Without Work*, Cambridge University Press, 1938

J.B. Priestley, *Angel Pavement*, Heinemann, 1930 *English Journey*, Heinemann, 1934

M. Spring Rice, *Working Wives*, Penguin, 1981

B. Seebohm Rowntree, *Poverty and Progress*, Longman, 1941

K. Watkins, *Britain Divided*, Nelson, 1963

M. Weir, *Best Foot Forward*, Hutchinson, 1972